Striptease

BIG BOOTY WOMEN

By **I LIKE BIG BUTTS**

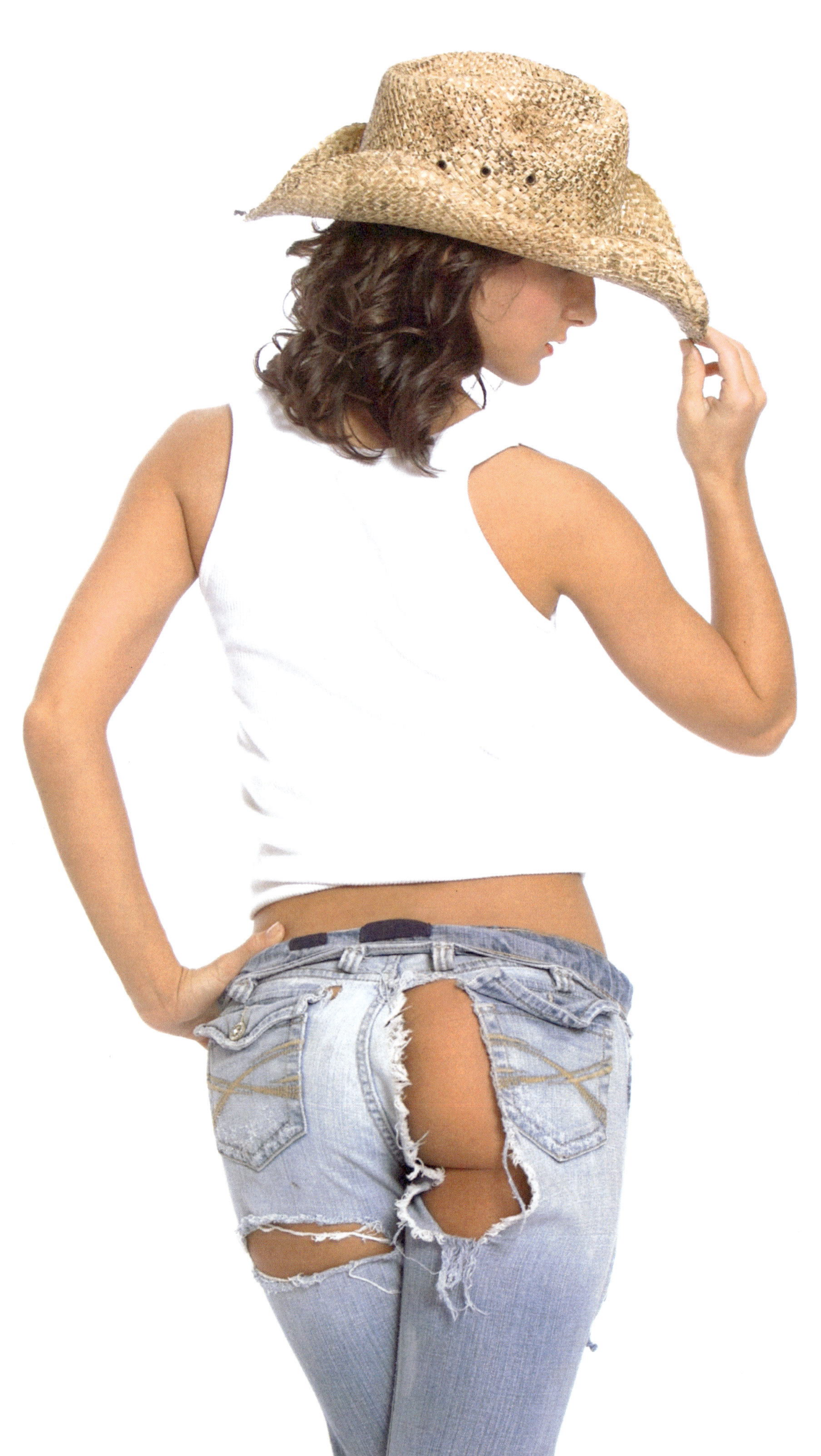

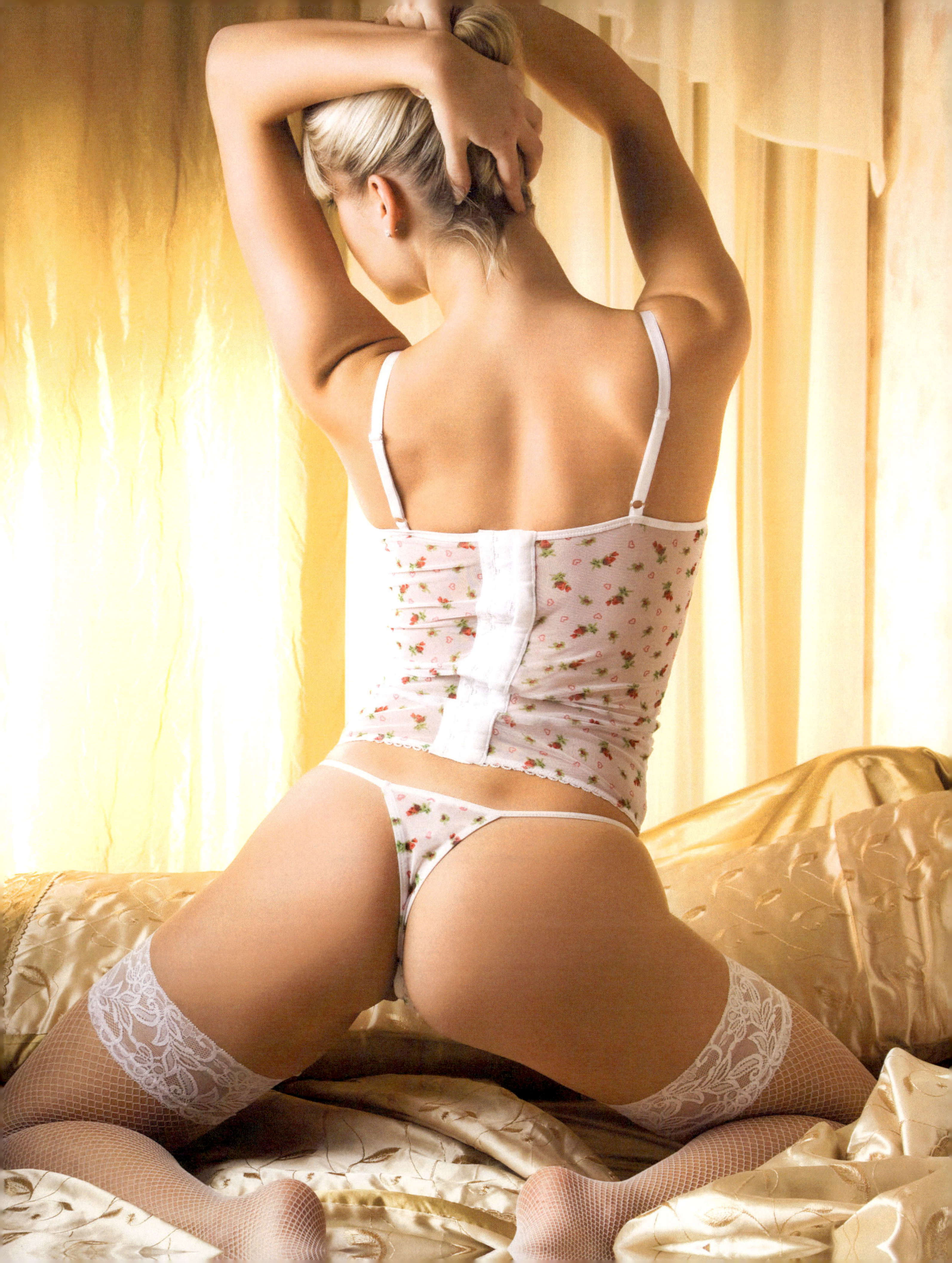

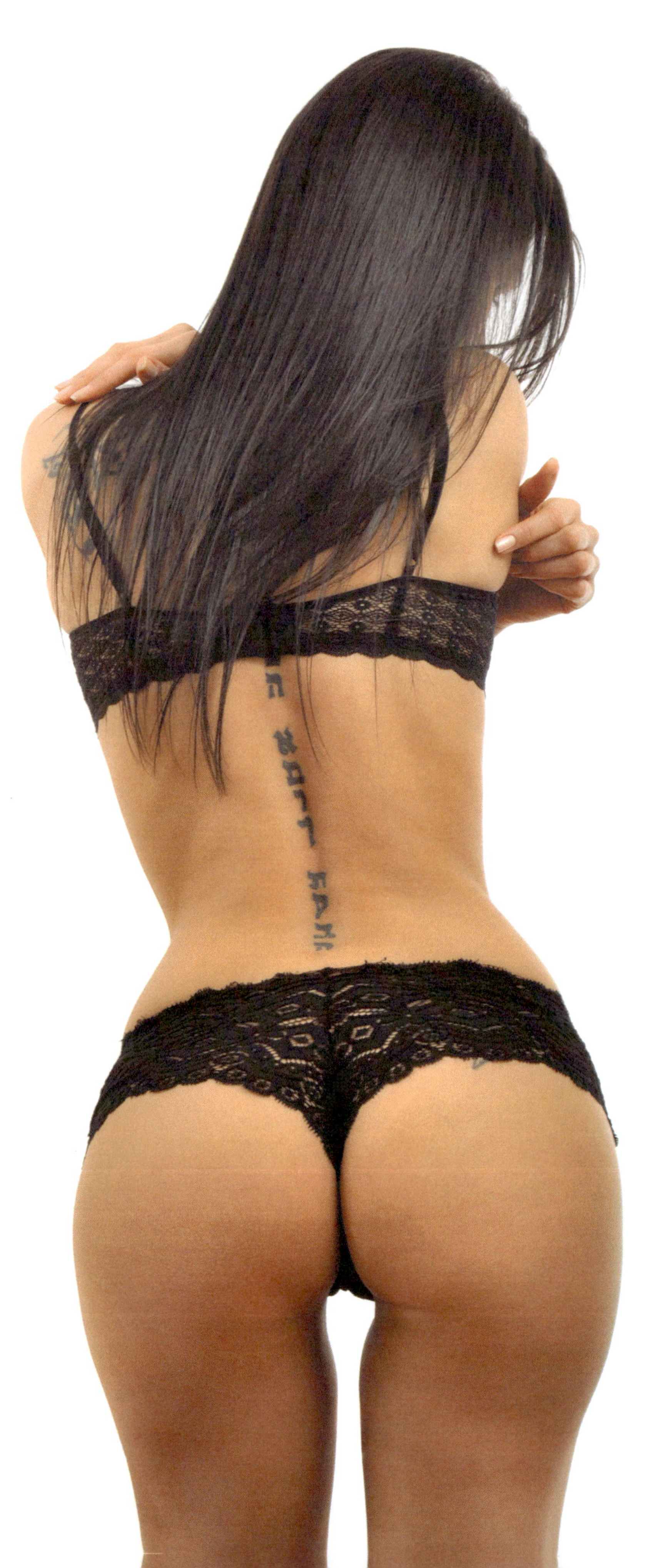

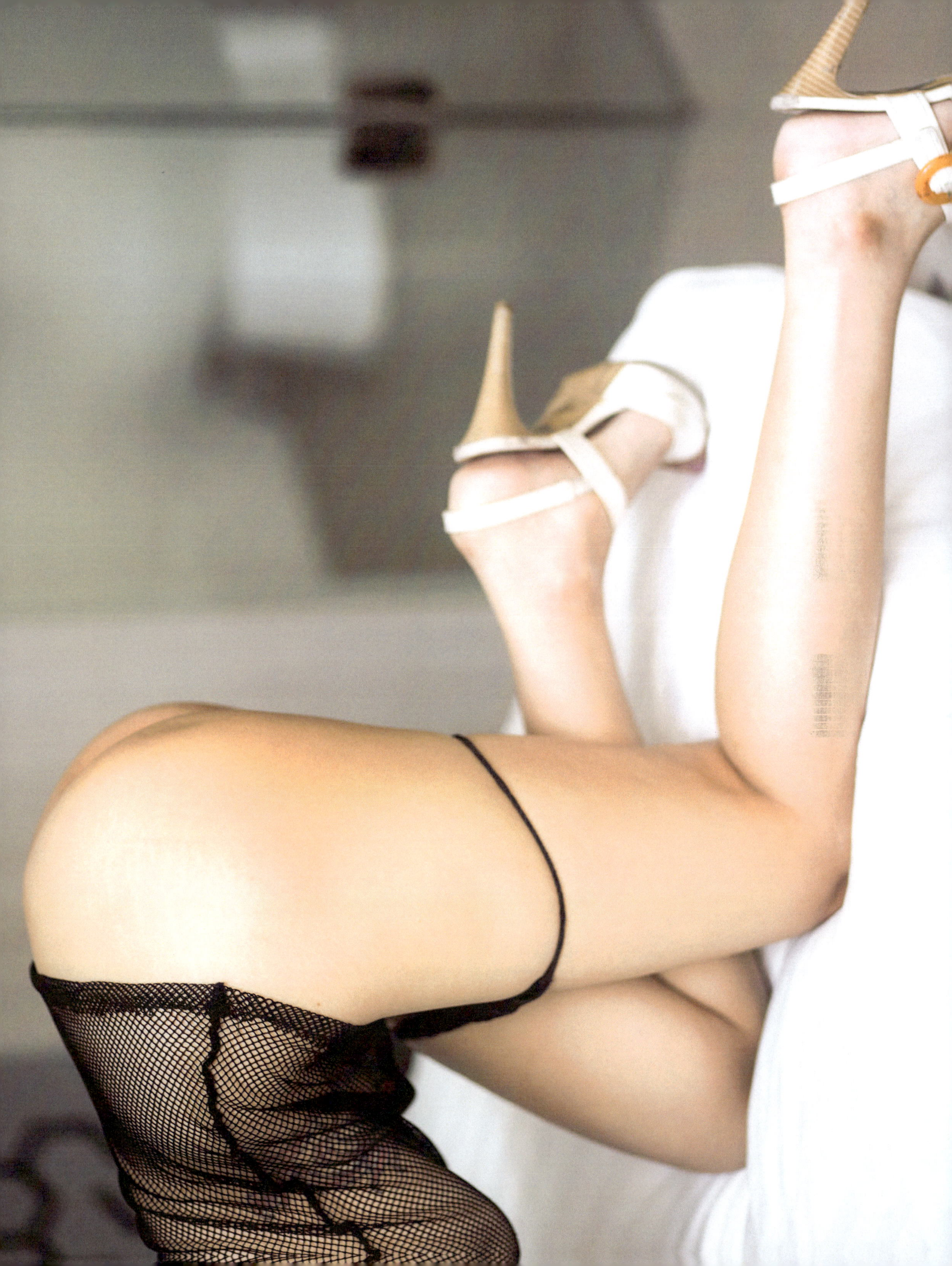

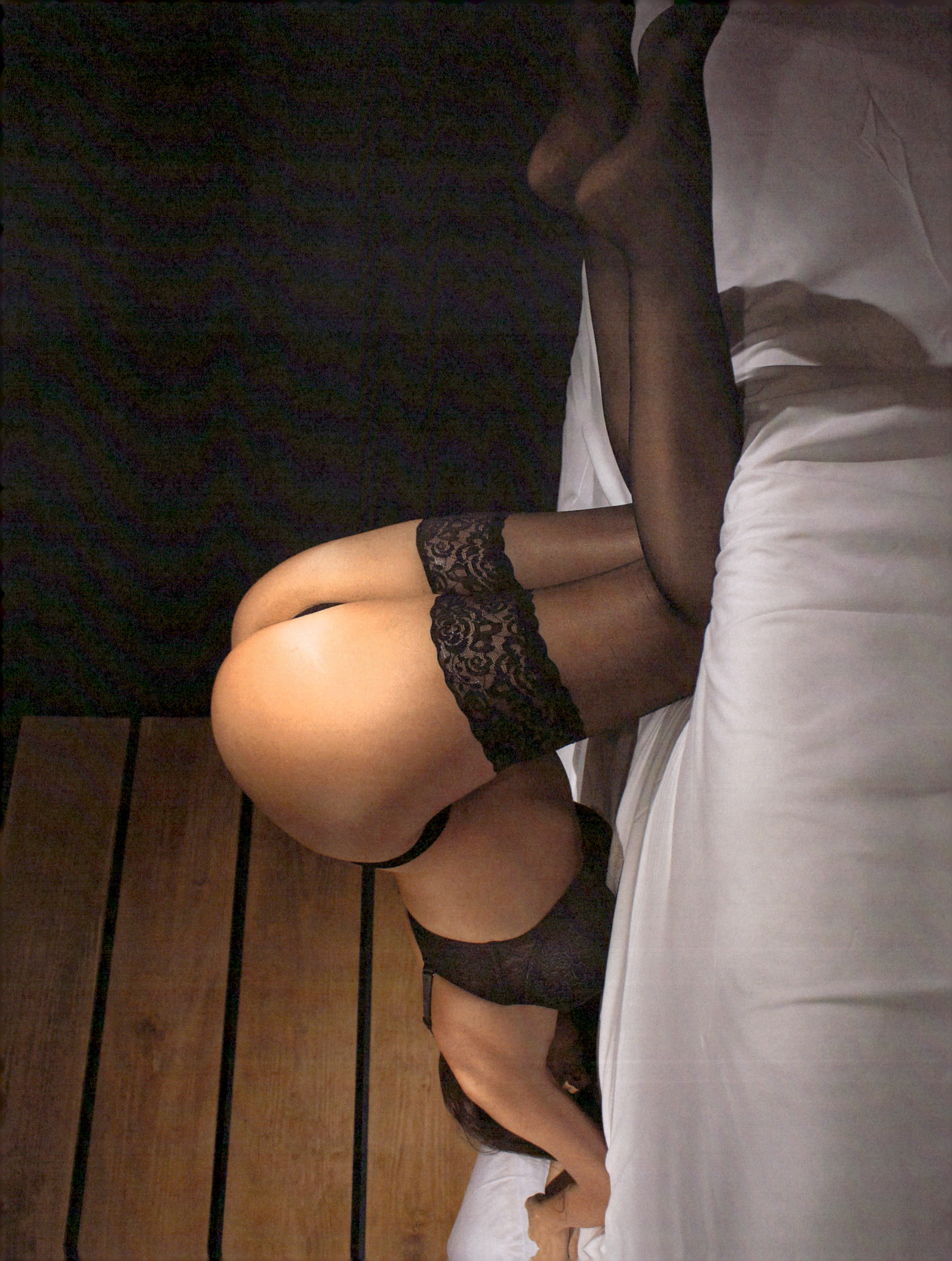

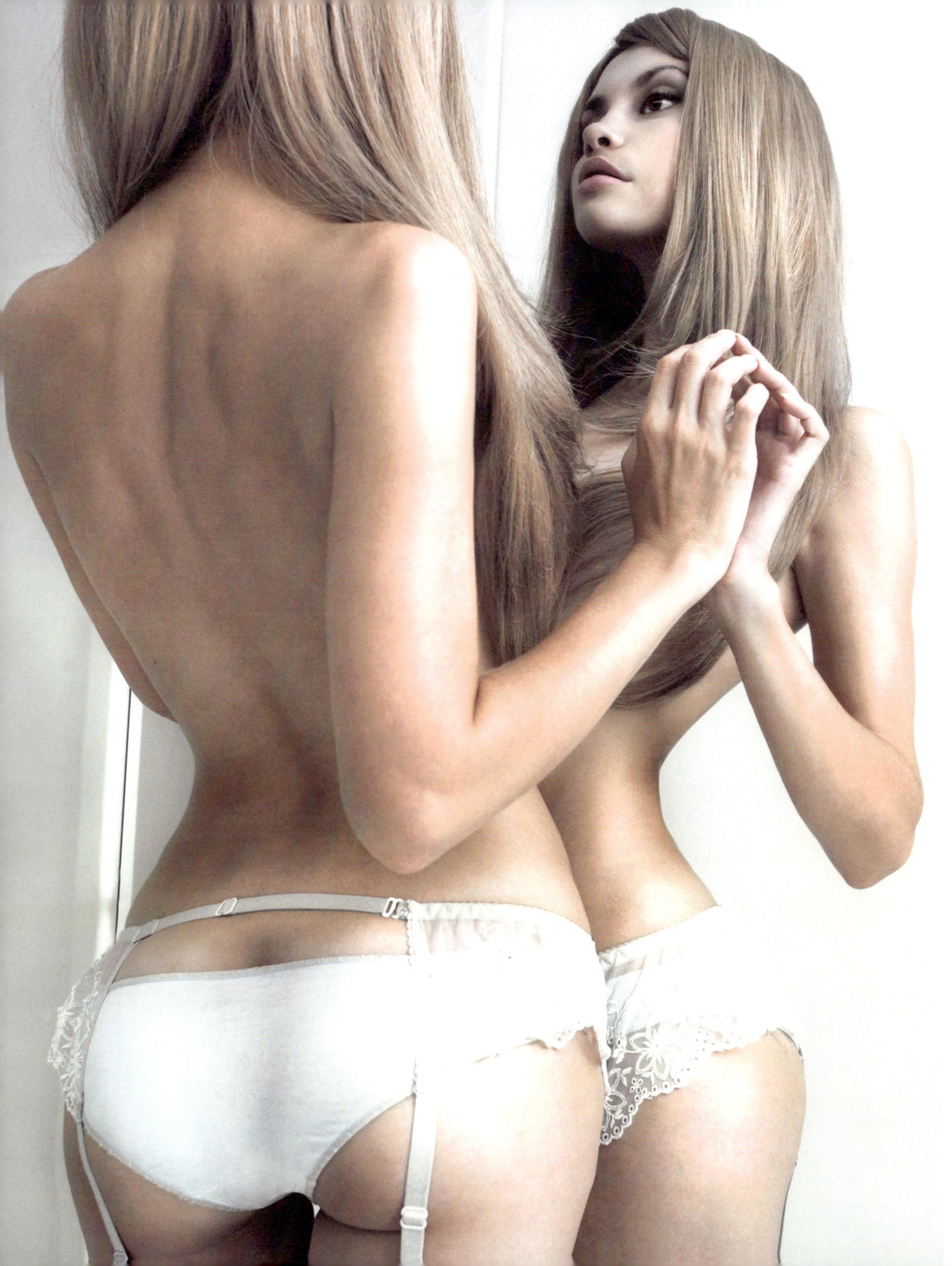

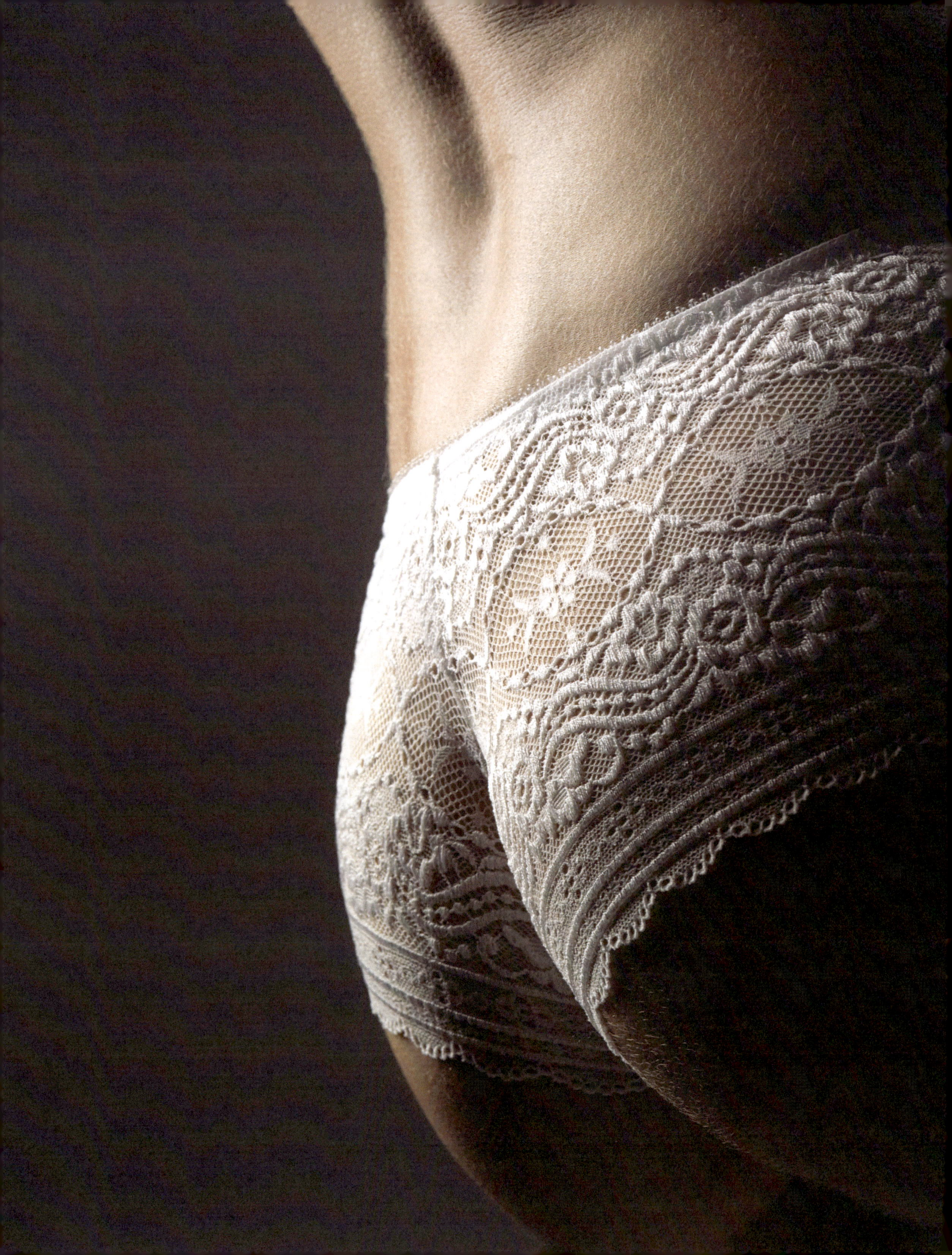

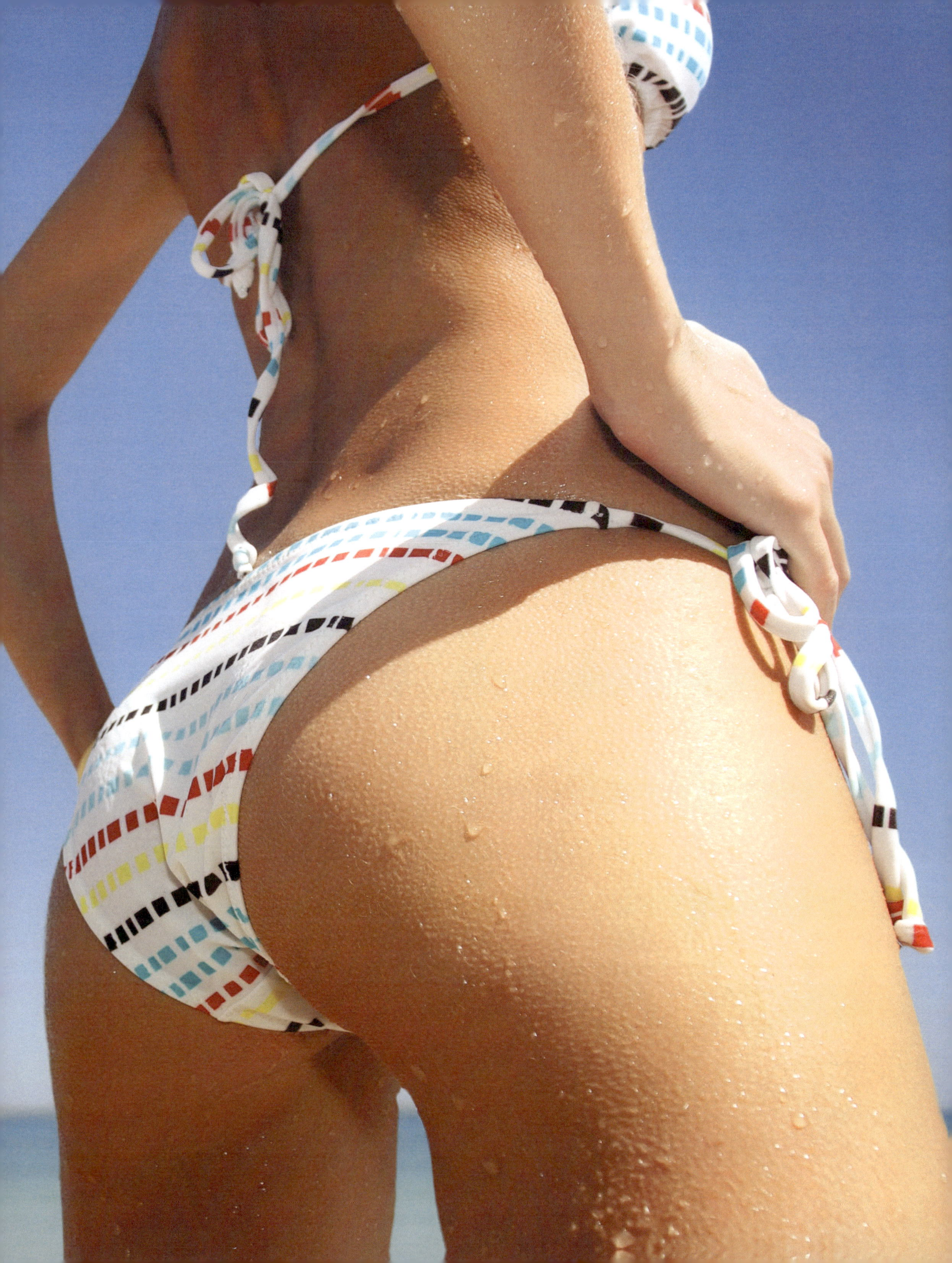

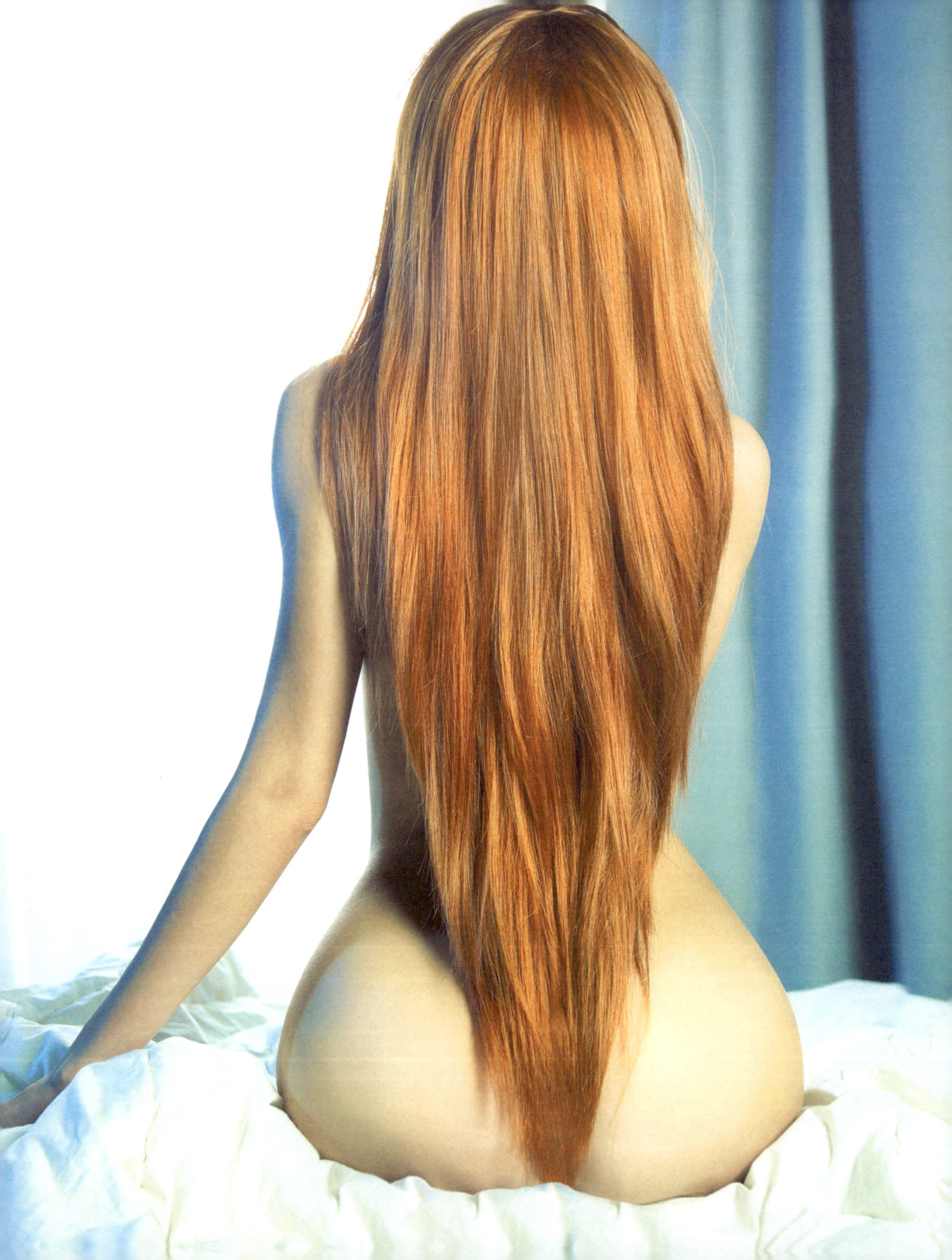

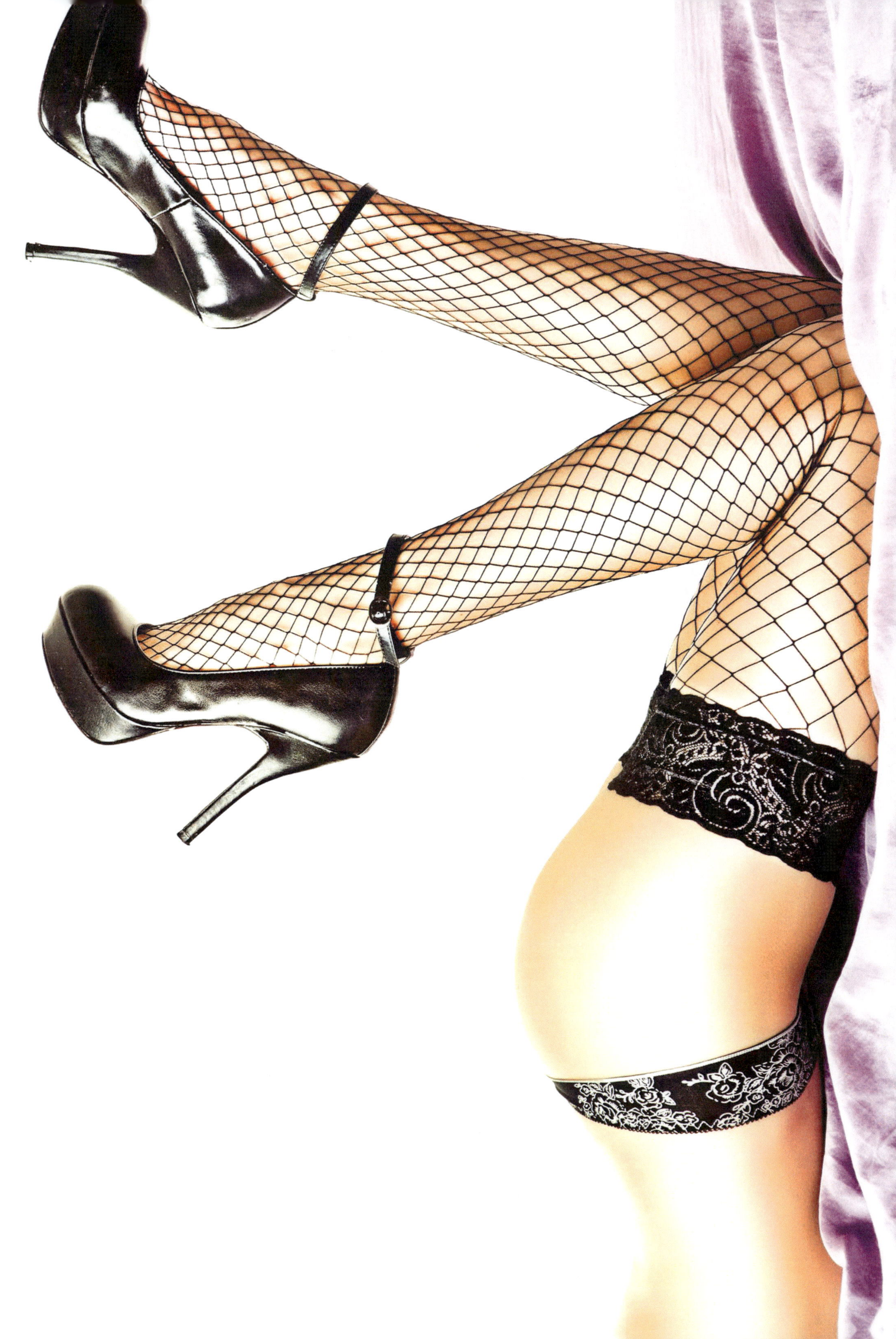

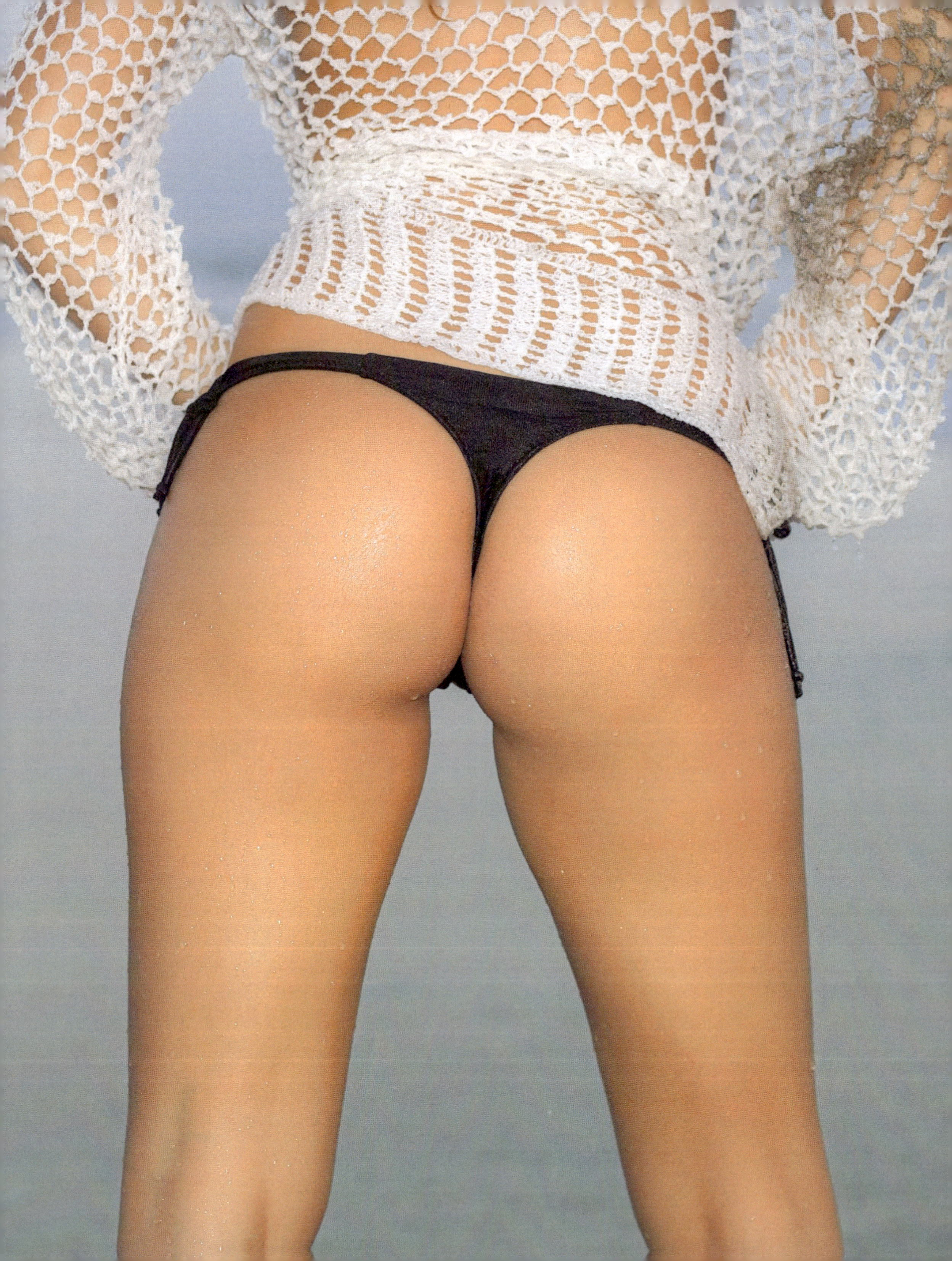

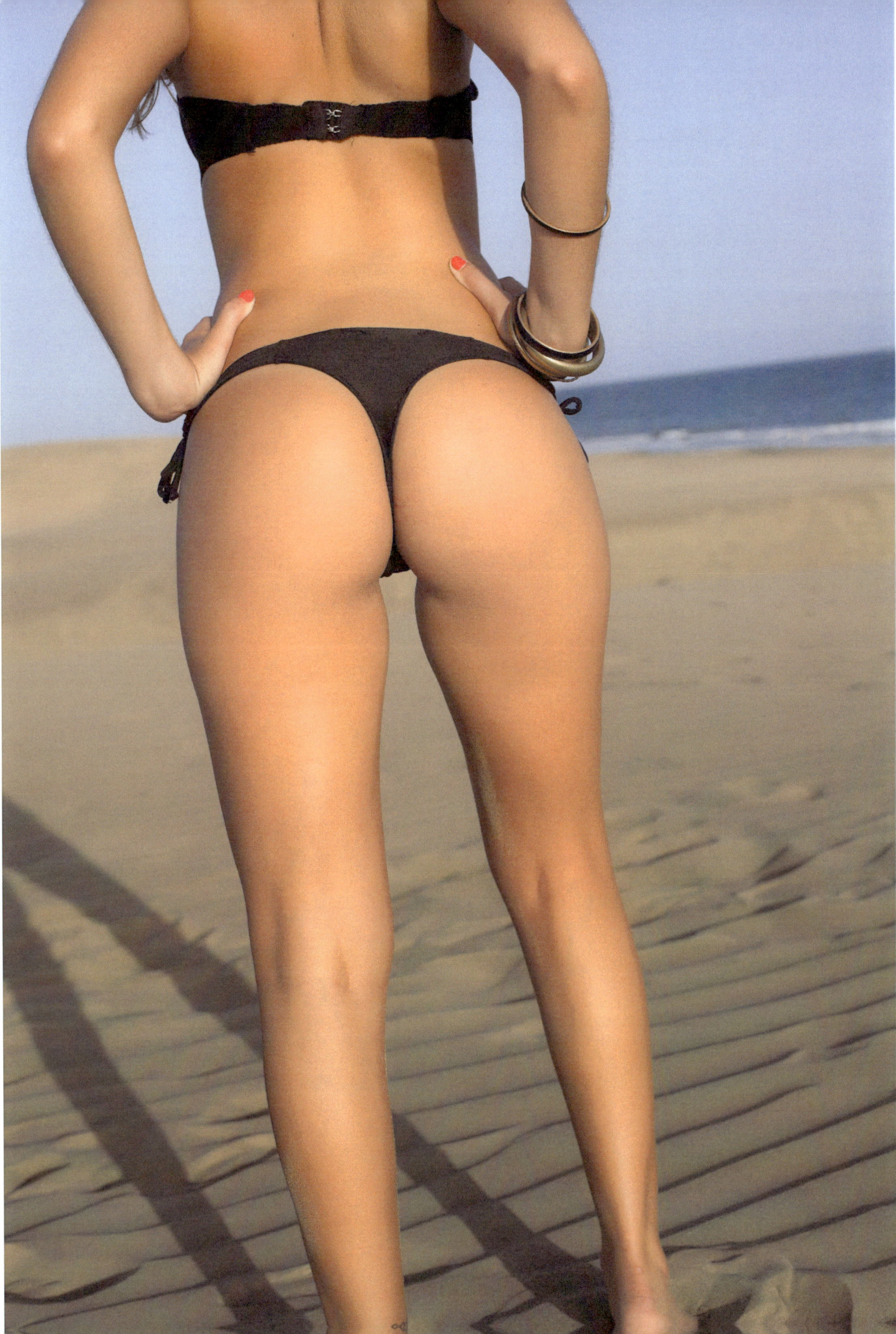

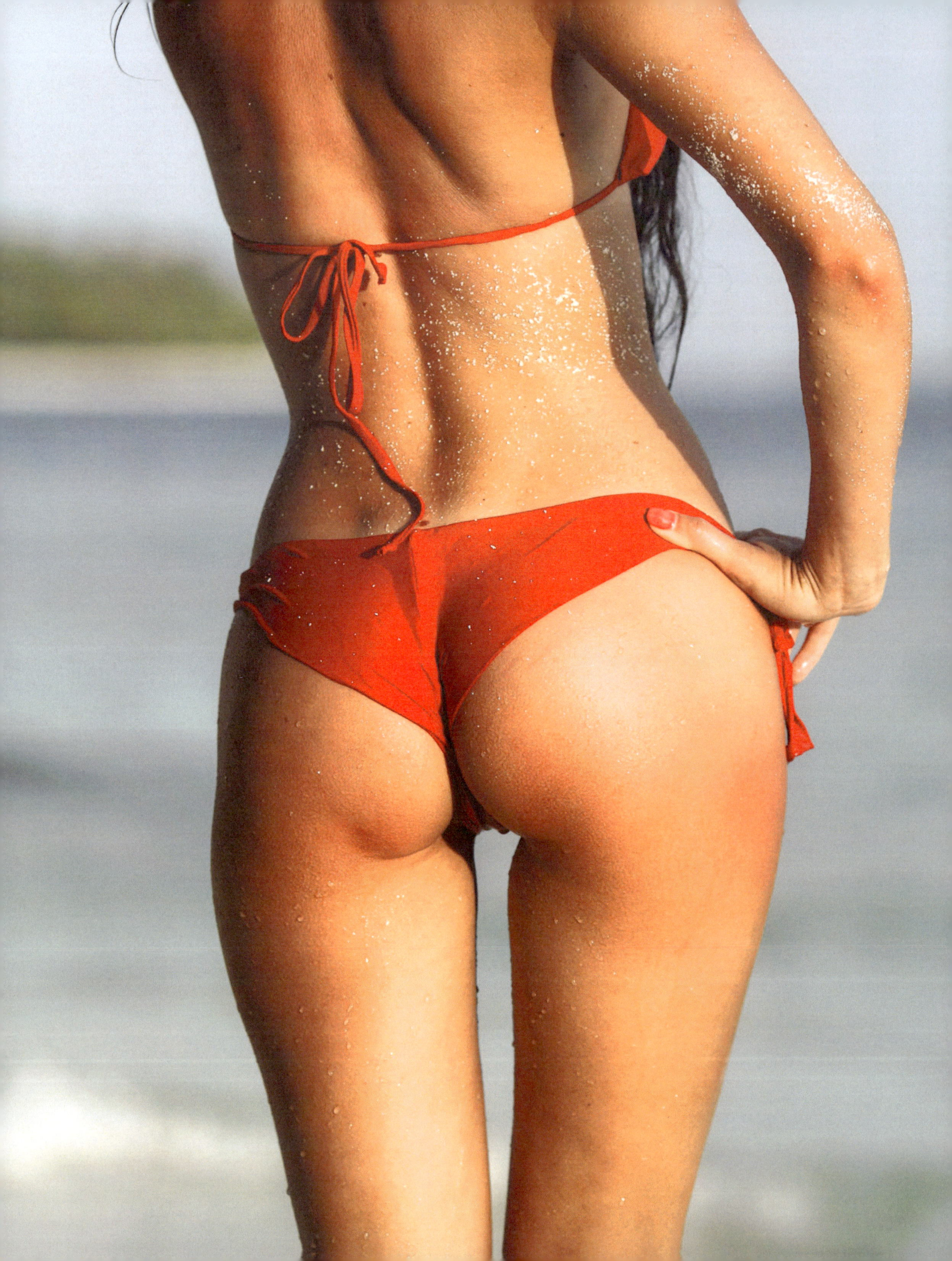

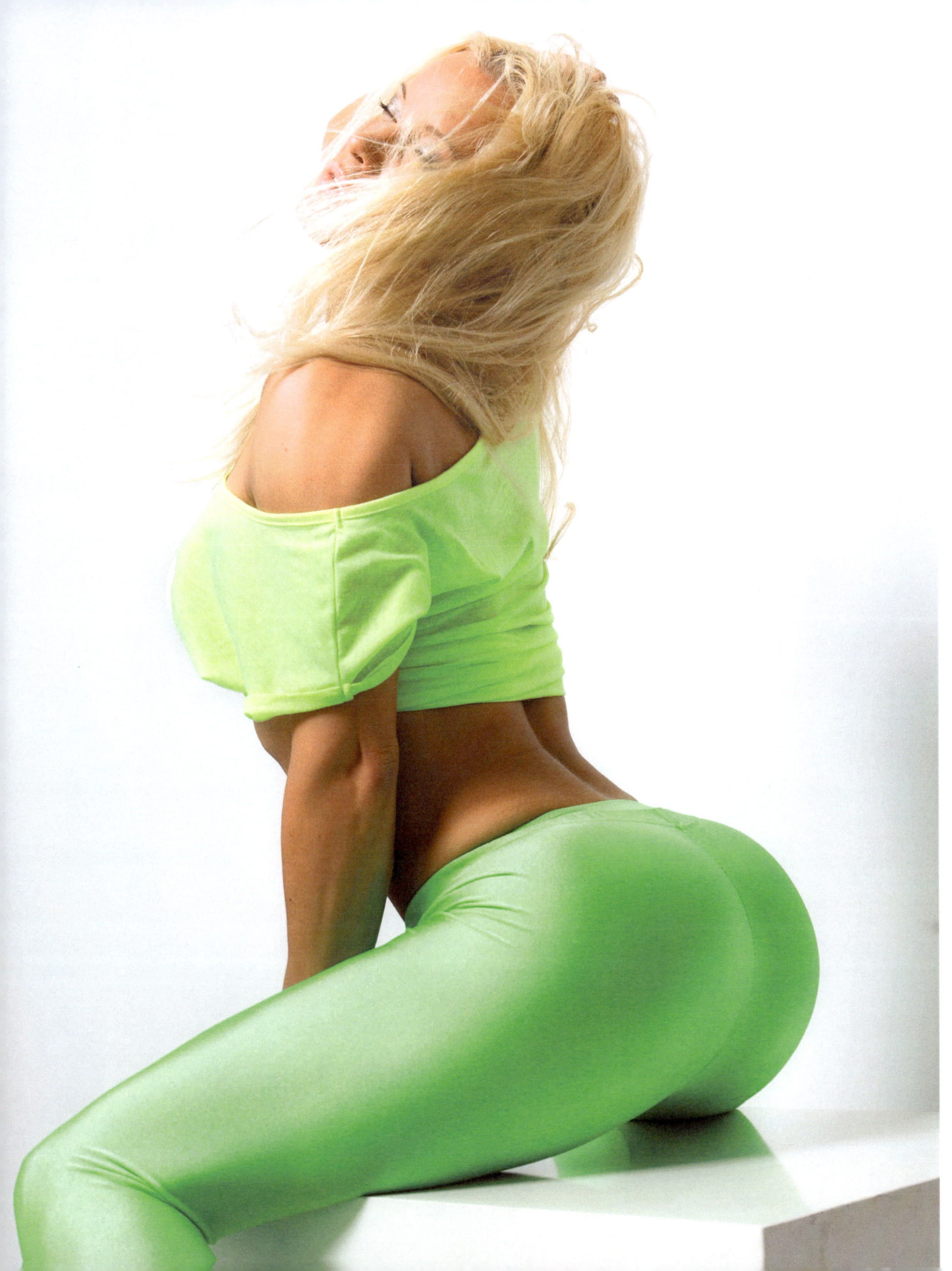

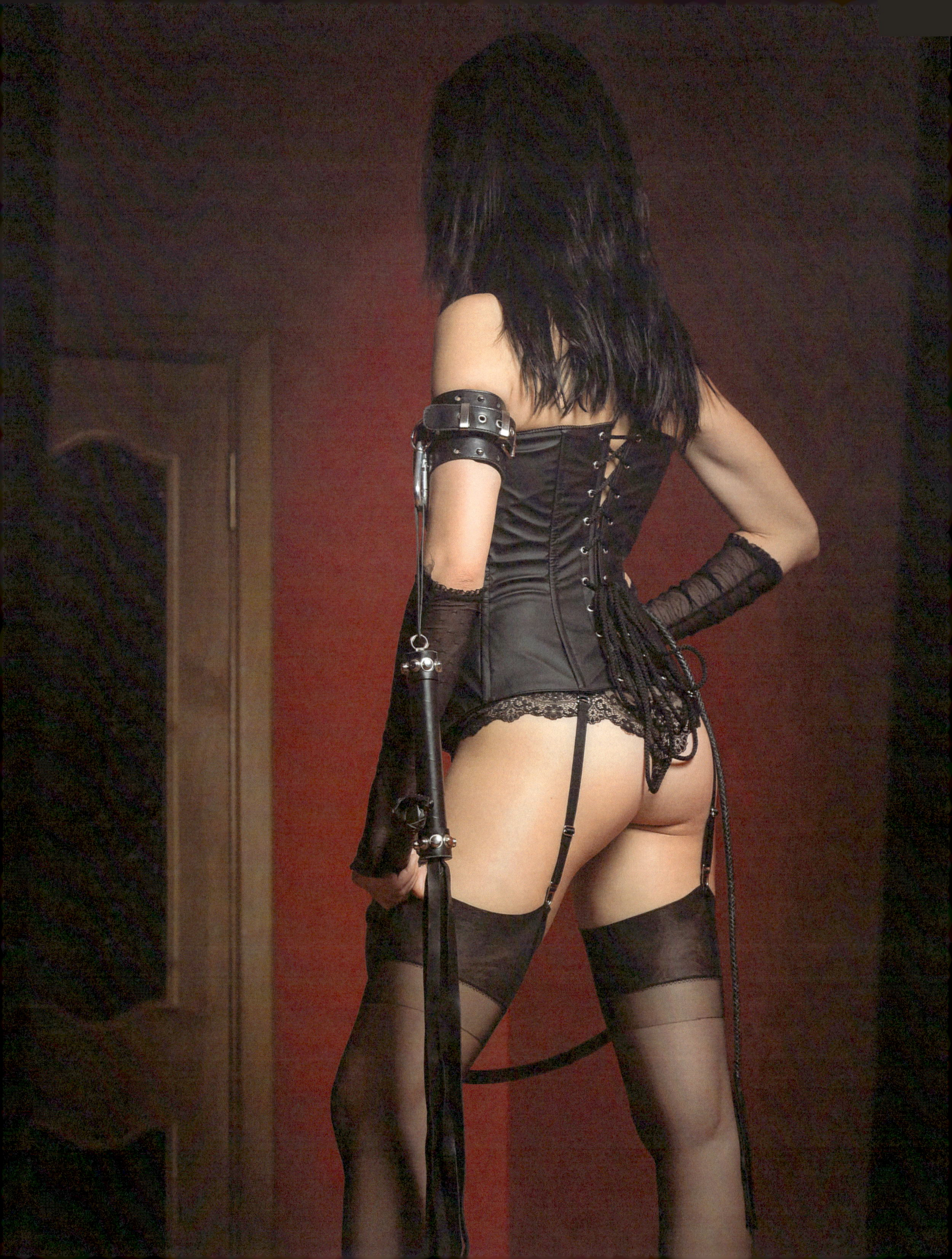

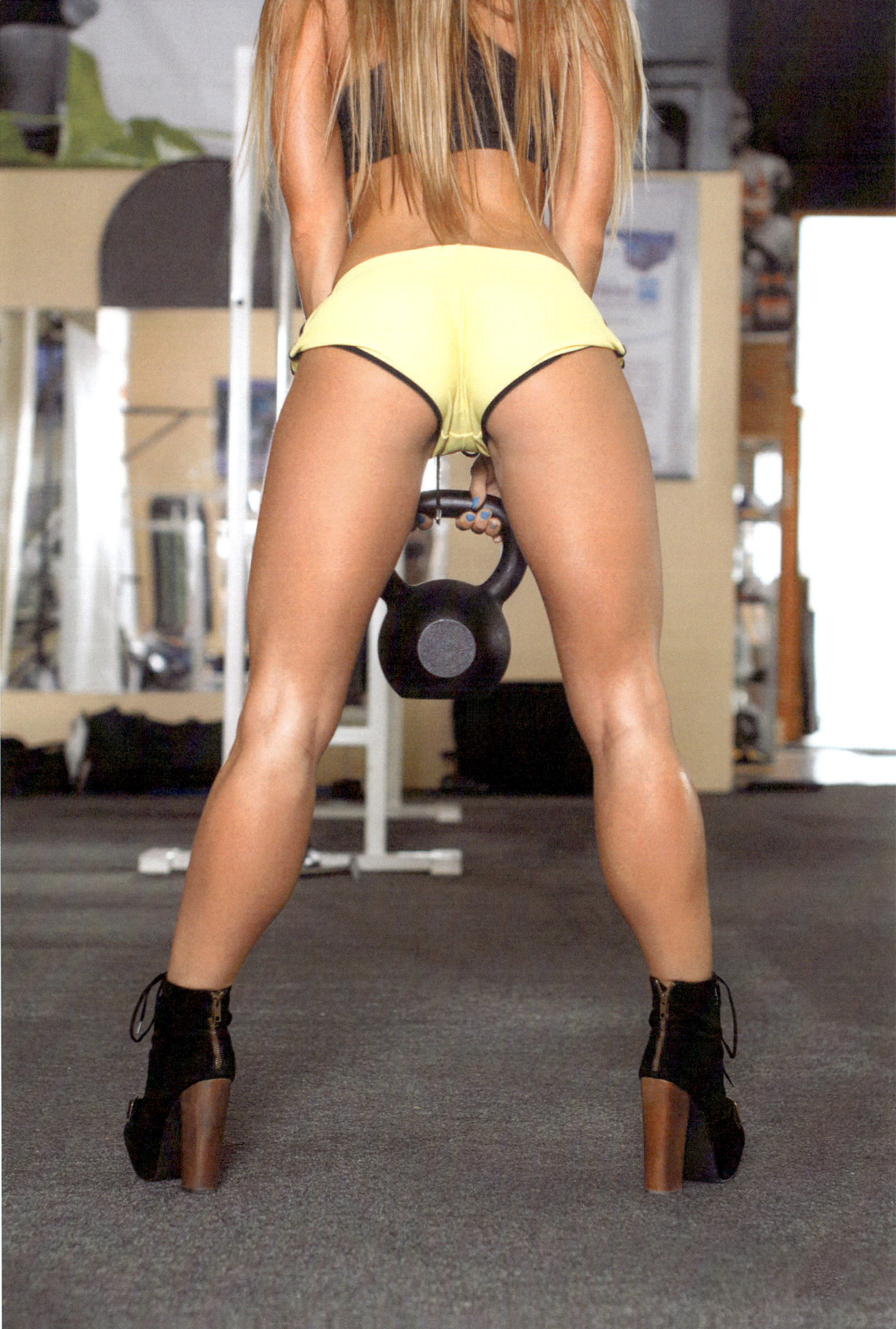

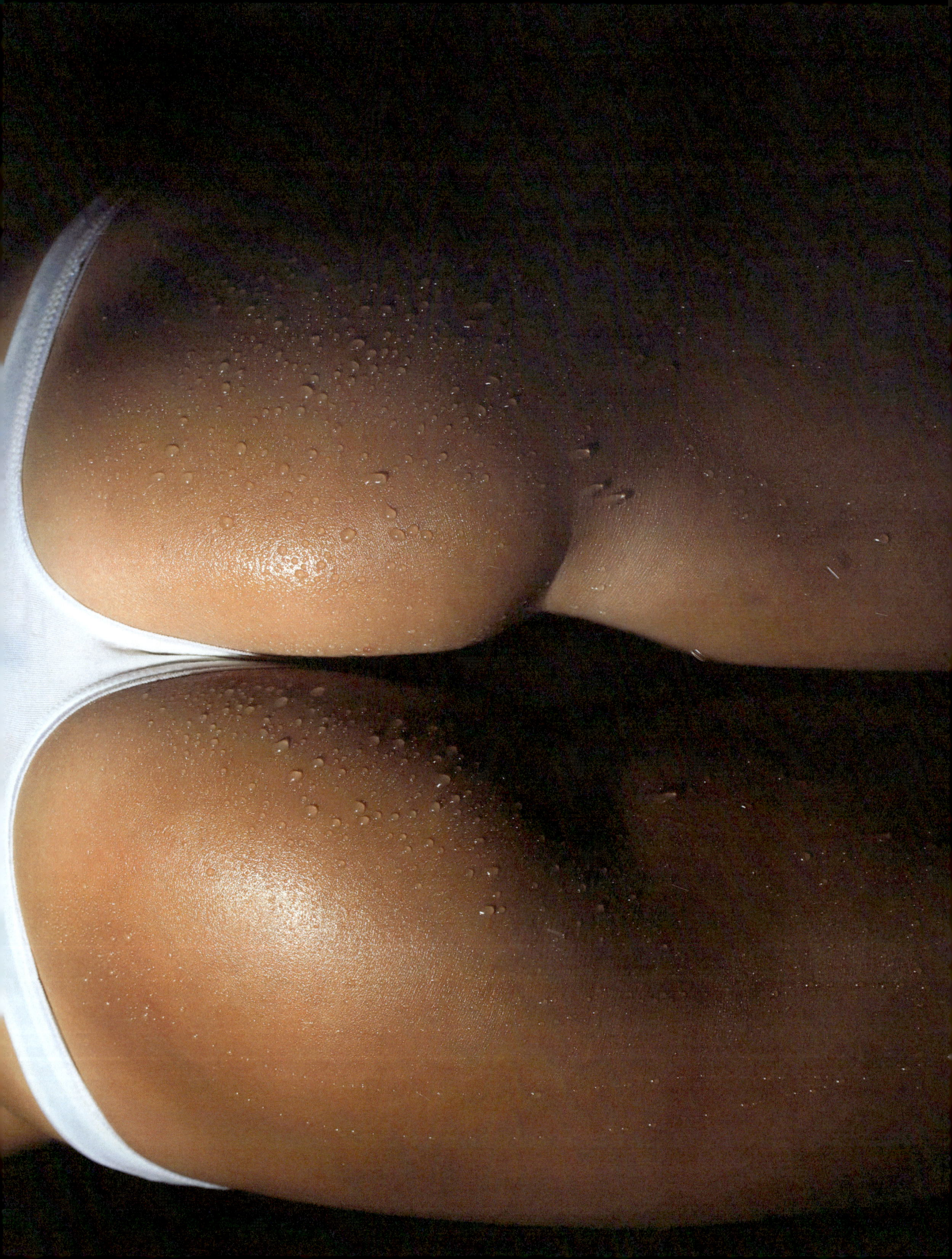

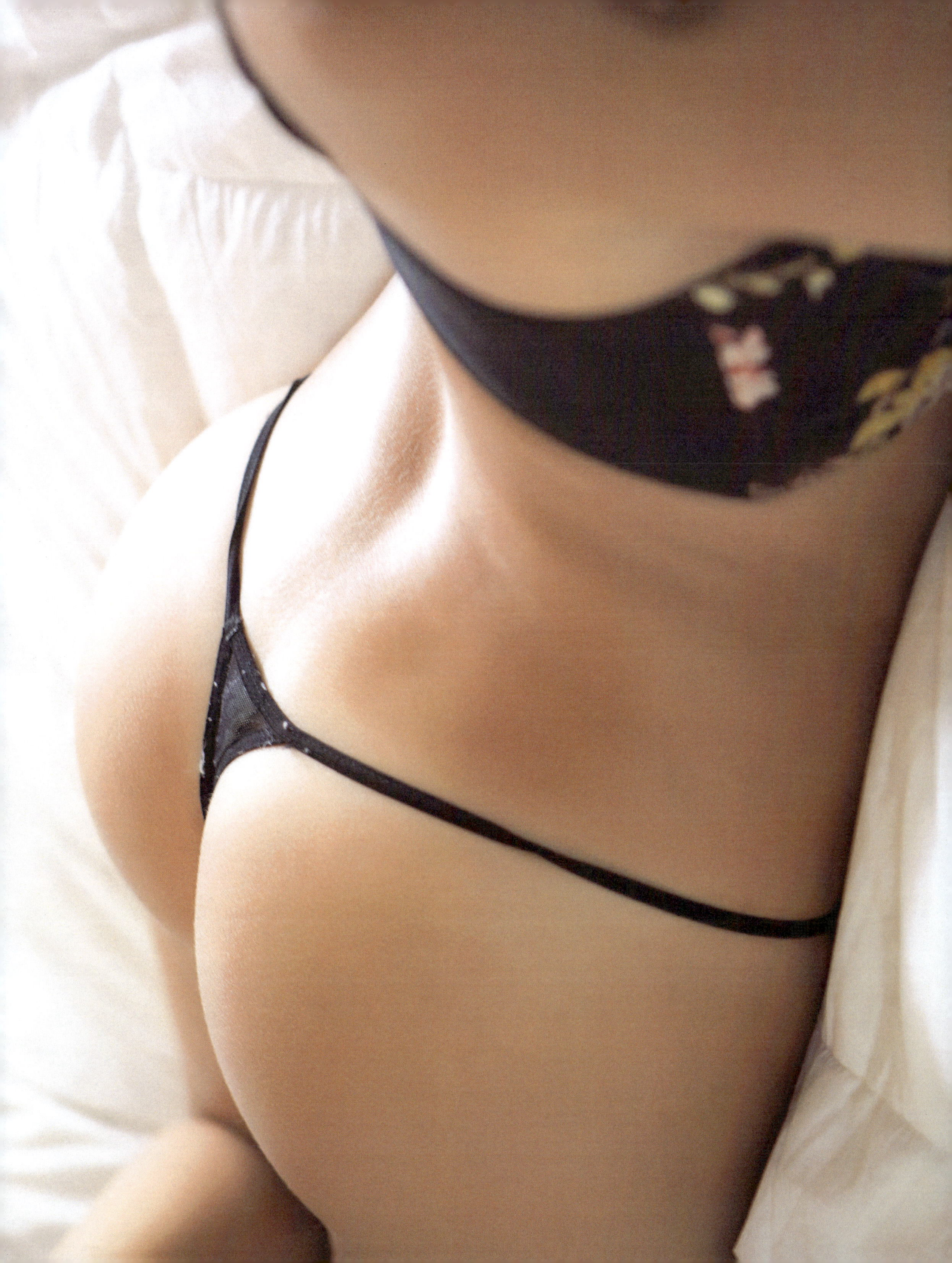

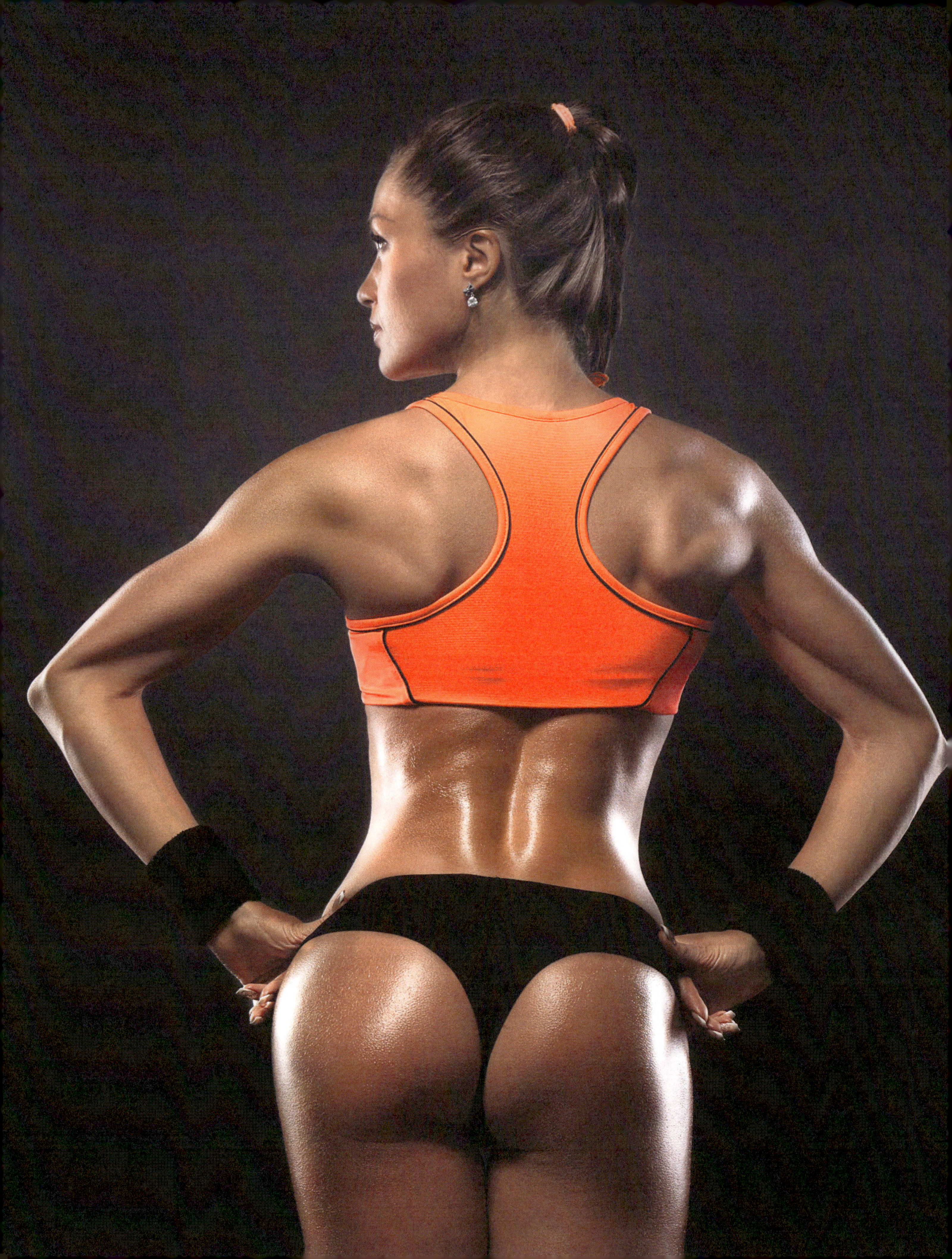

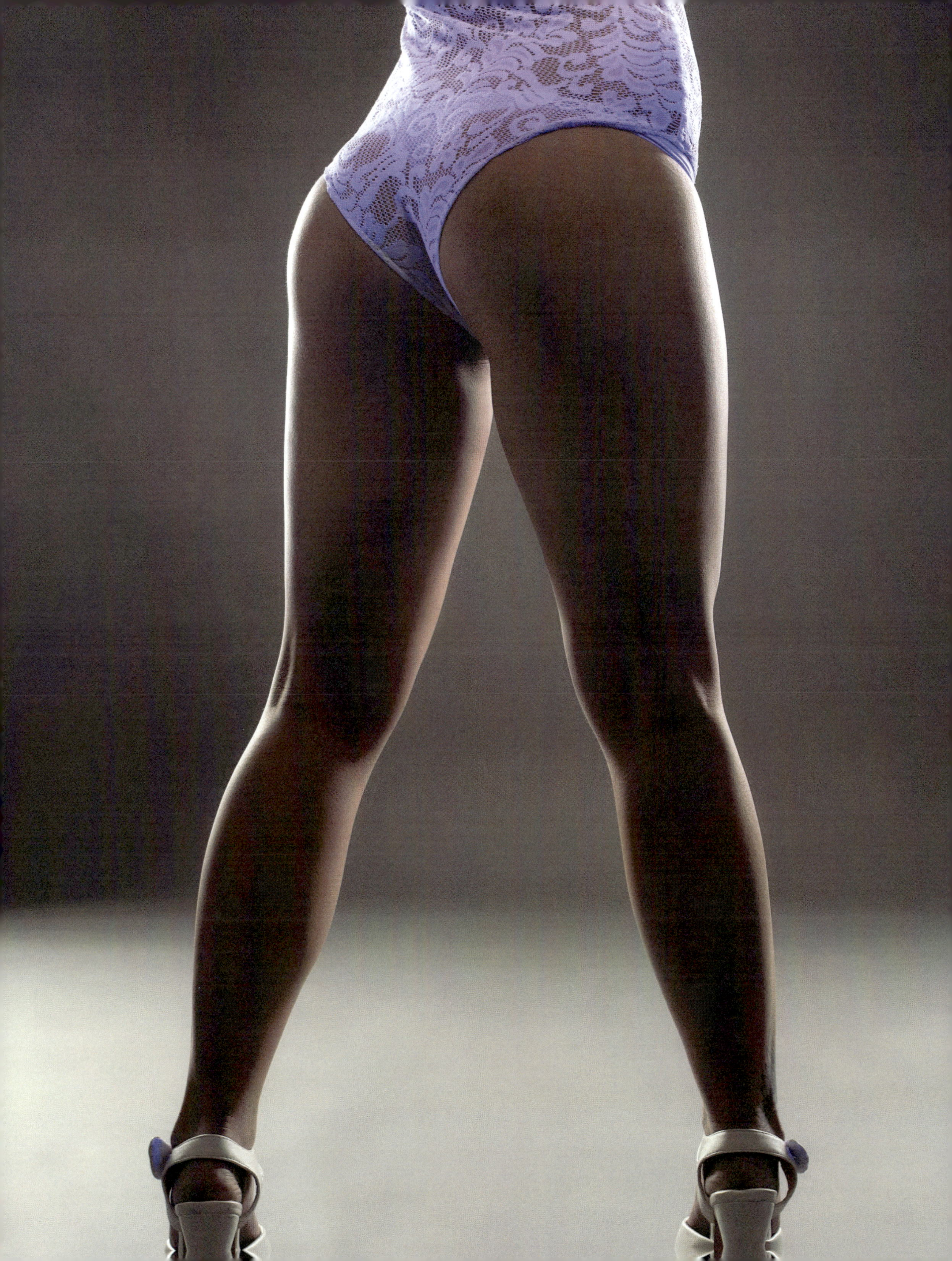

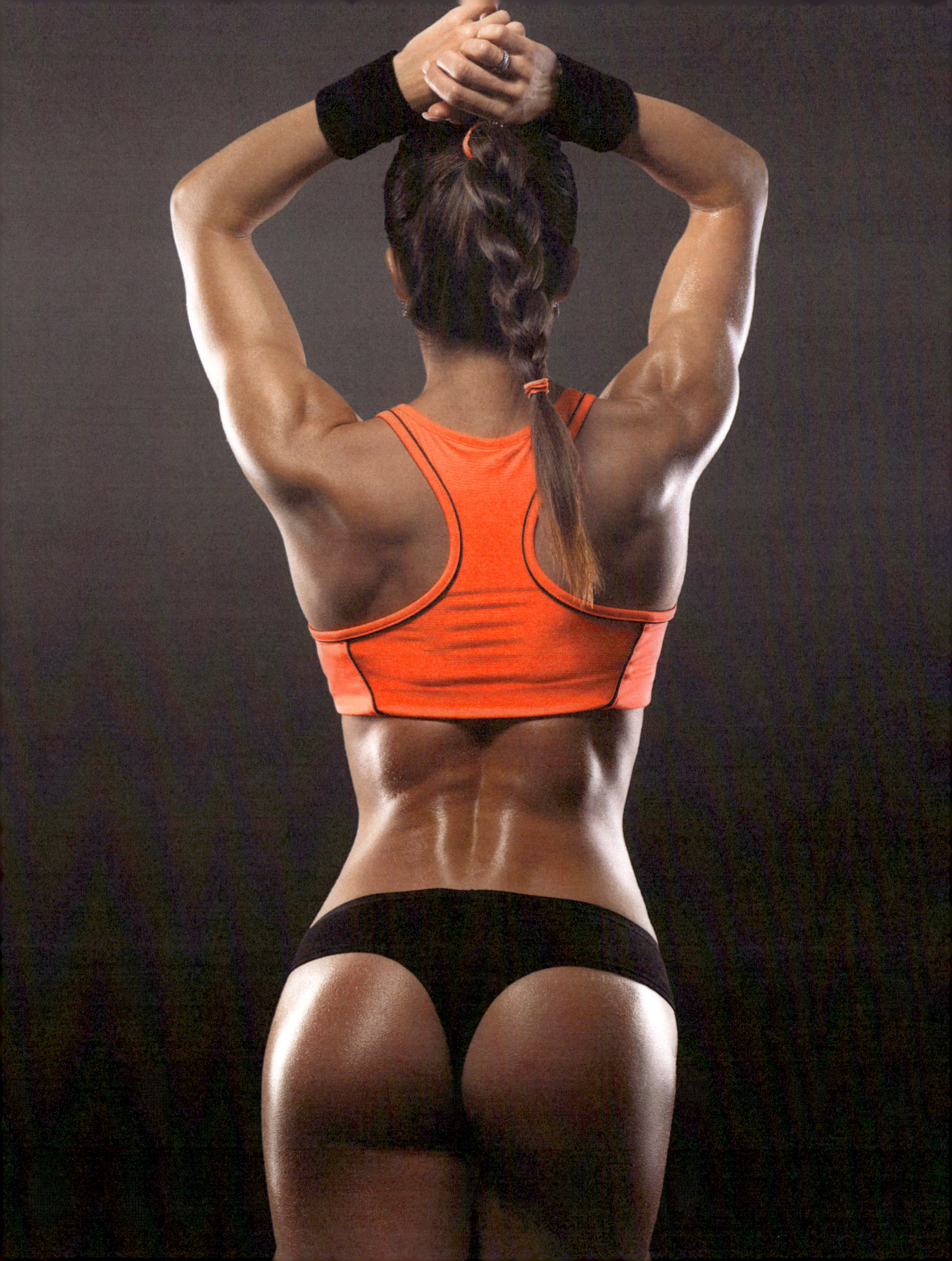

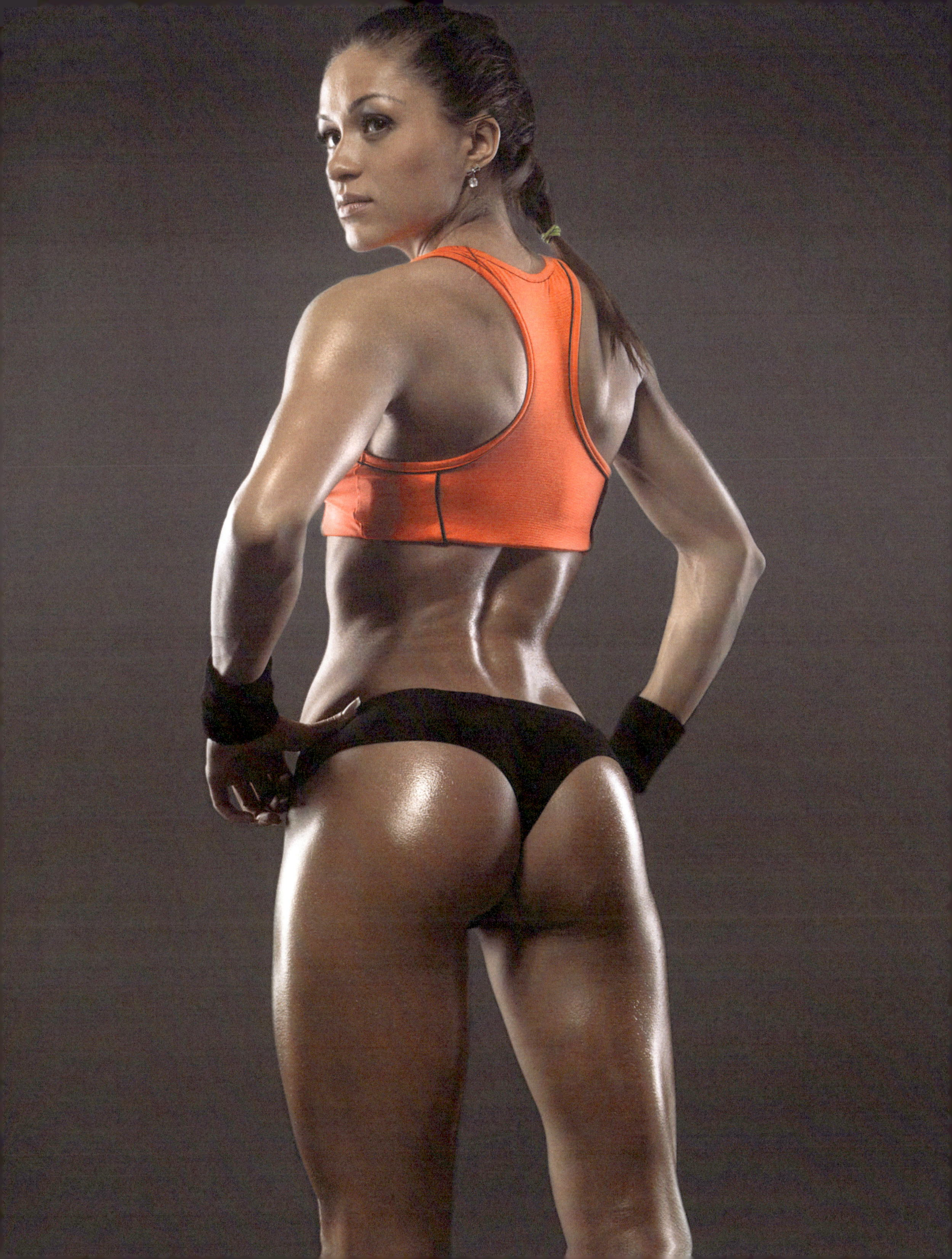

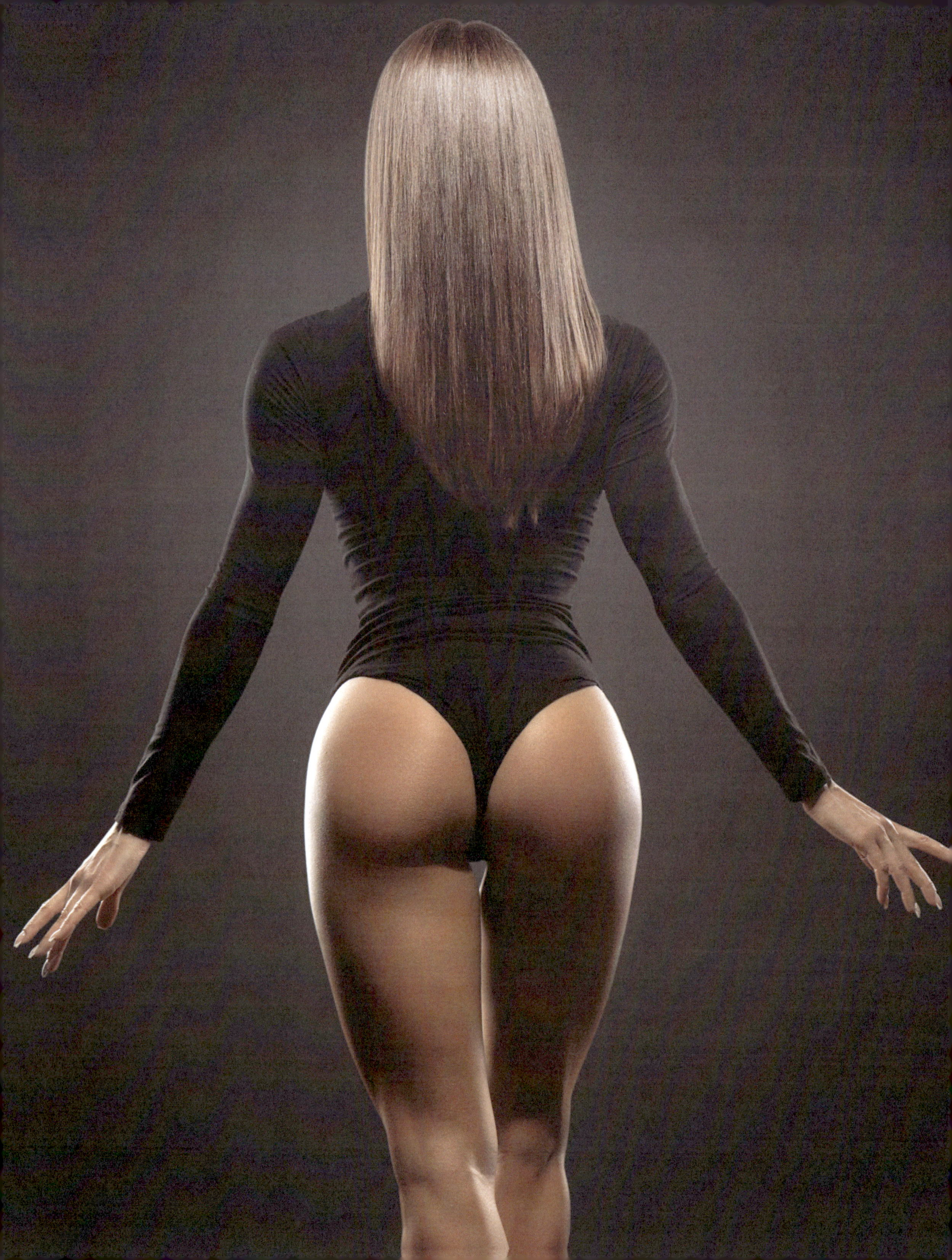

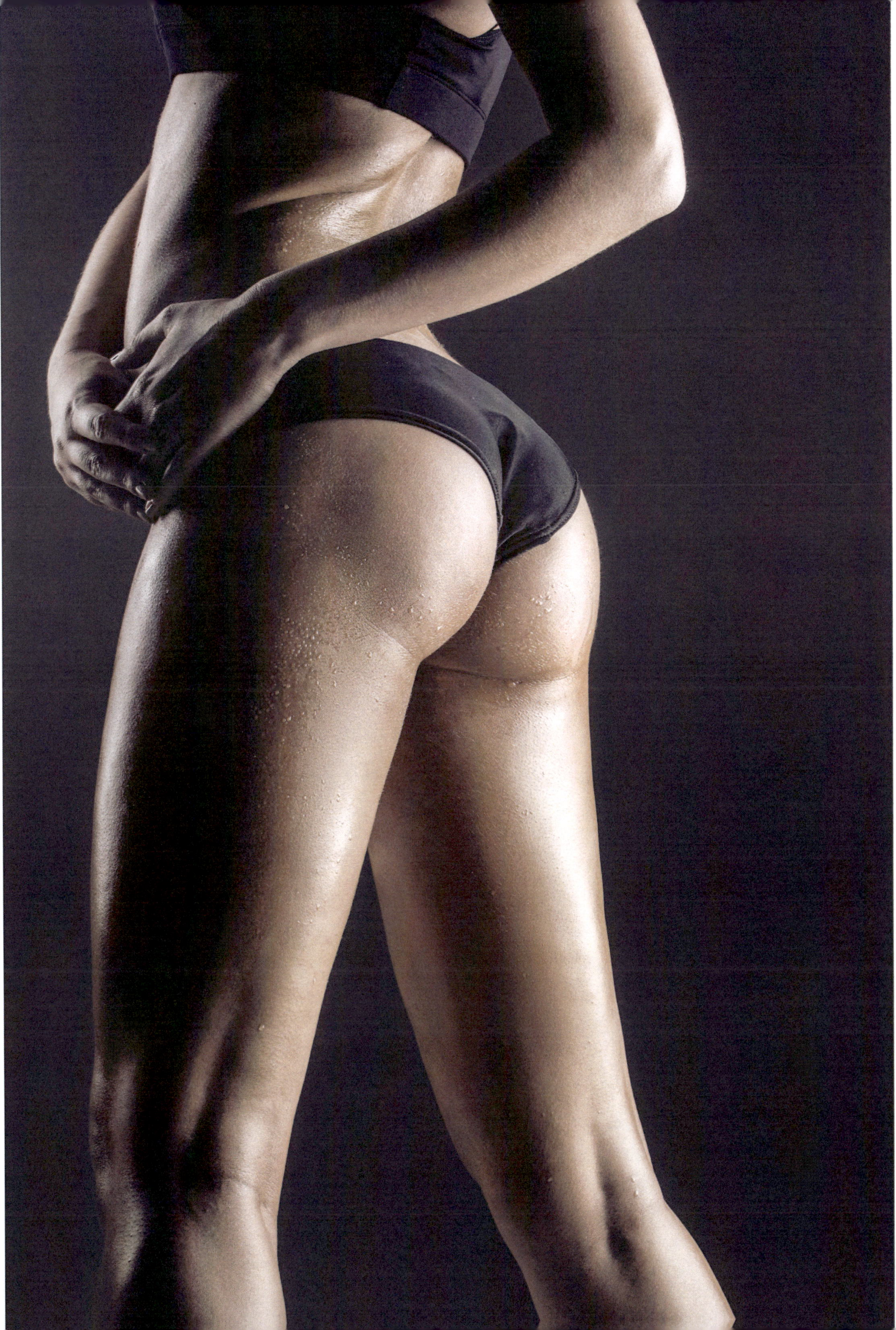

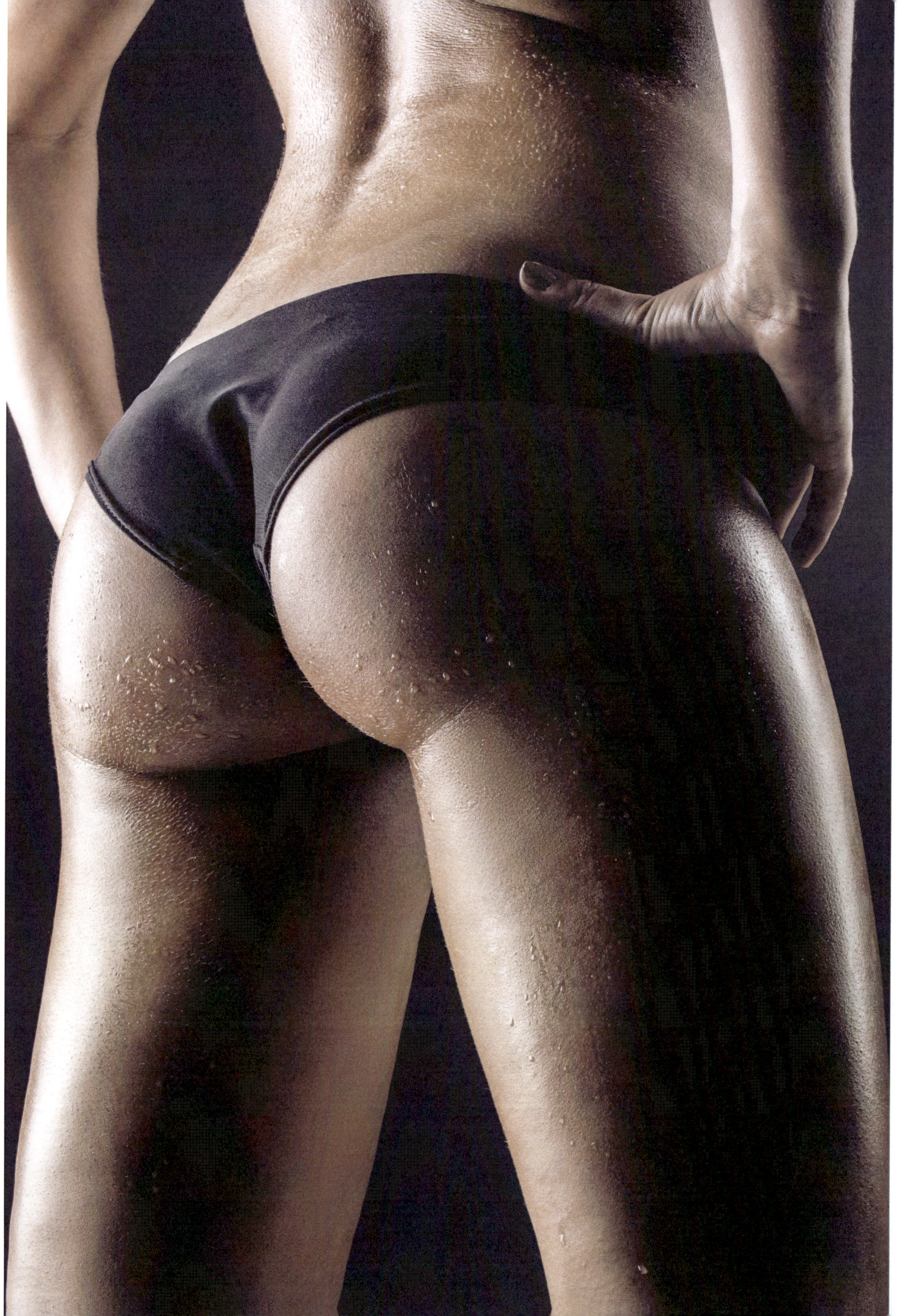

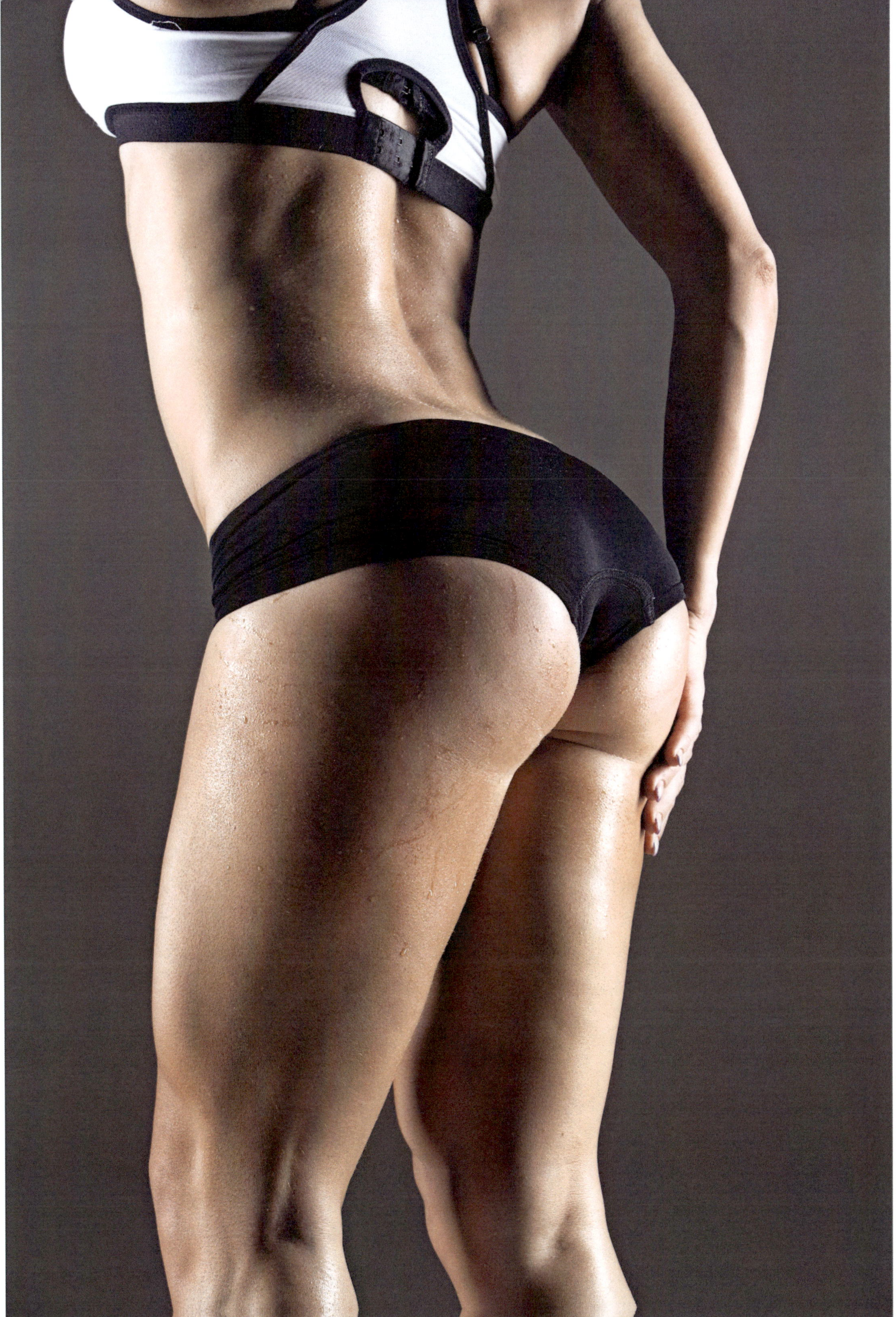

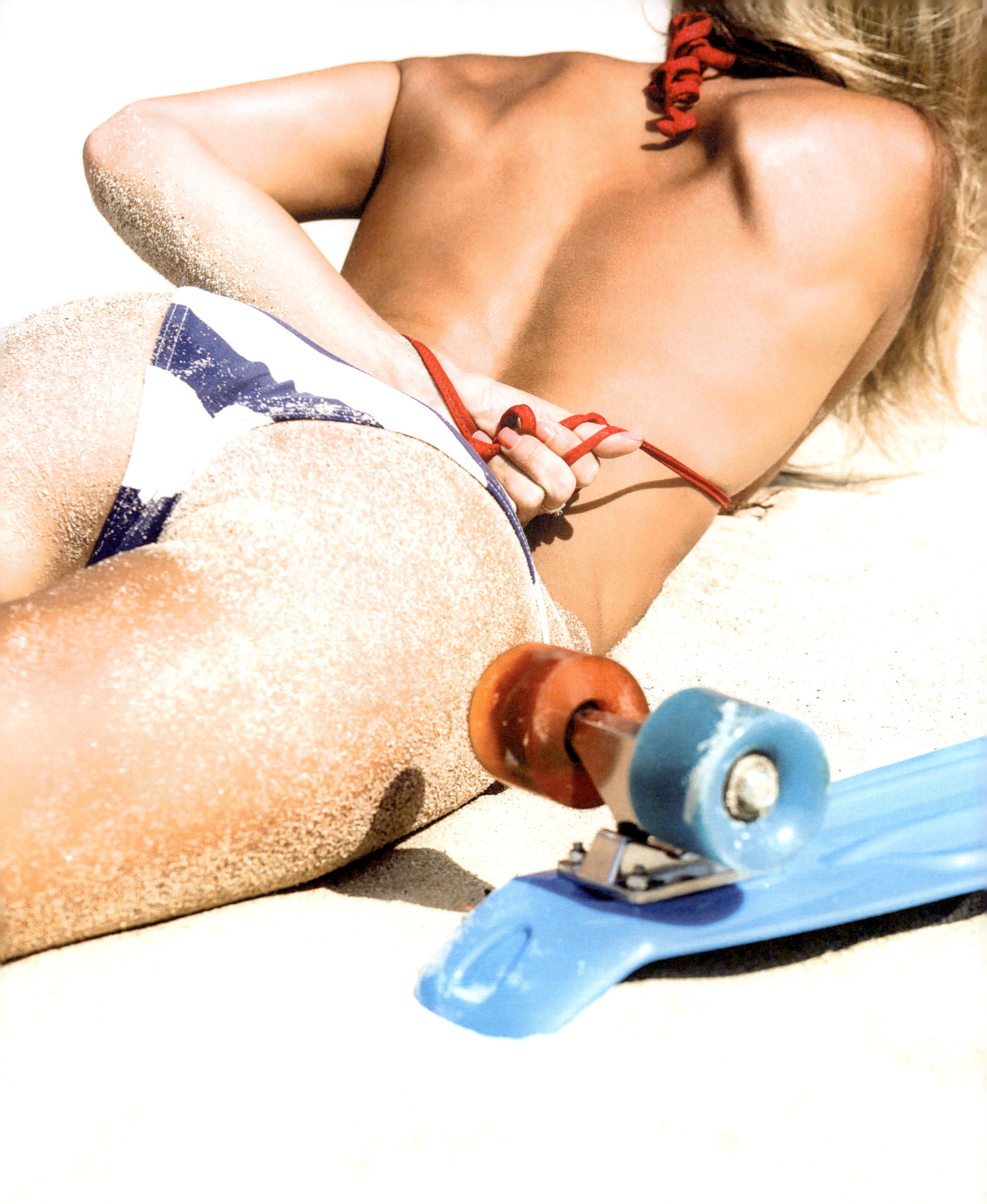

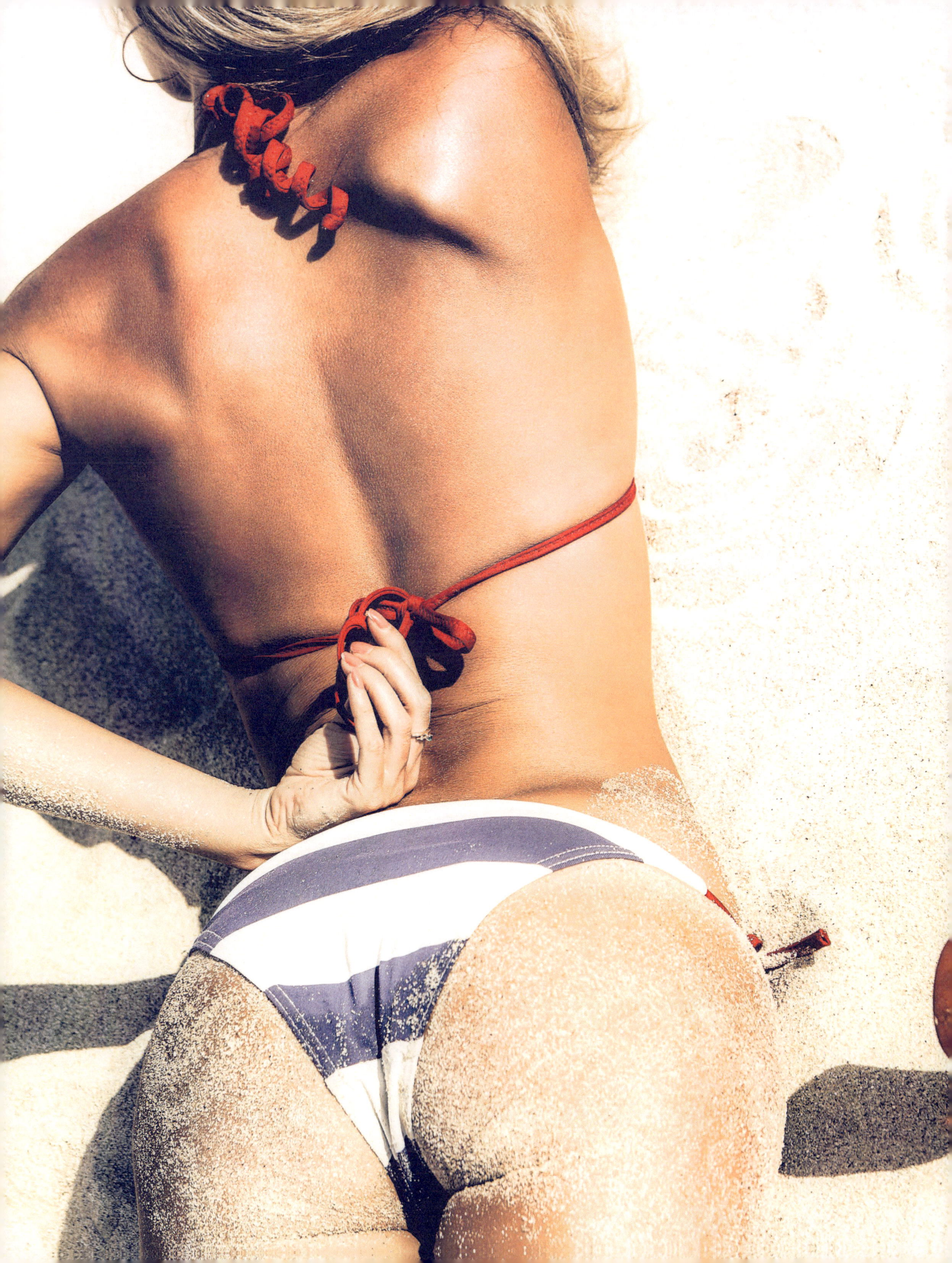

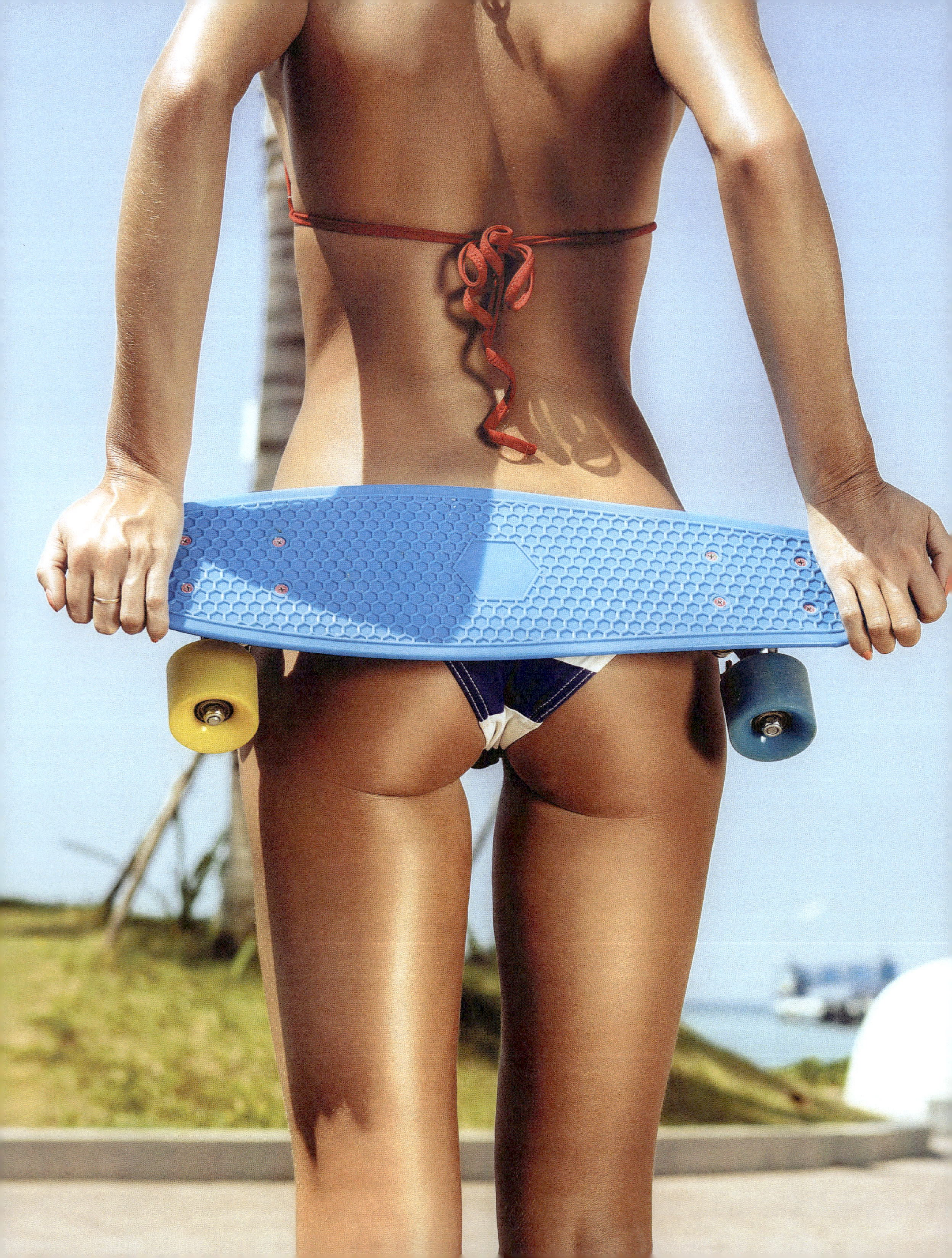

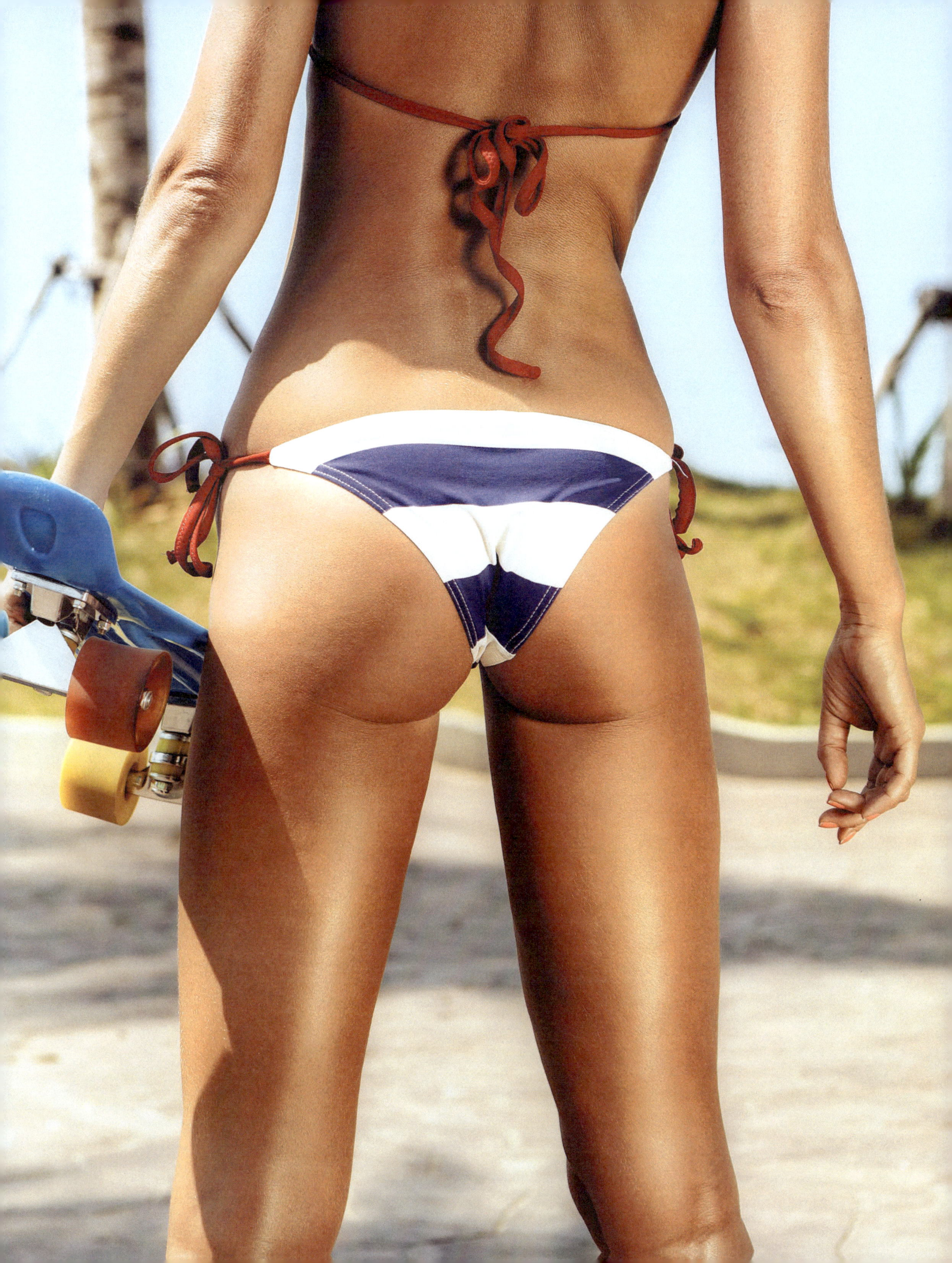

www.ingramcontent.com/pod-product-compliance
Ingram Content Group UK Ltd.
Pitfield, Milton Keynes, MK11 3LW, UK
UKRC032027290726
14090UKWH00008B/491